THE ANIMAL KINGDOM

LIFE IN THE WILD

ELIZABETH OAKLEY

Editorial planning
Jollands Editions

SCHOOLHOUSE PRESS, *Inc.*

Original copyright, © Macmillan Education Limited 1986
© BLA Publishing Limited 1986

Designed and produced by BLA Publishing Limited,
Swan Court, East Grinstead, Sussex, England.
Also in LONDON · HONG KONG · TAIPEI · SINGAPORE · NEW YORK
A Ling Kee Company

Illustrations by Steve Lings/Linden Artists,
 Dick Twinney/Linden Artists and BLA Publishing Limited
Color origination by Chris Willcock Reproductions
Printed in Italy by G. Canale & C. S.p.A. — Torino

86/87/88/89   6 5 4 3 2 1

Photographic credits

t = top b = bottom l = left r = right

cover: Aquila

4 Anthony Bannister/NHPA; 5 Ed Lawrenson; 6 Peter
Johnson/NHPA; 7t Aquila; 9 J & M Bain/NHPA; 12
John Shaw/NHPA; 13b Ivan Polunin/NHPA; 14 Michael
Leach/NHPA; 15b Aquila; 16, 17 Seaphot; 20t Douglas
Baglin/NHPA; 20b ZEFA; 21 L.H. Newman/NHPA; 23
Philip Wayre/NHPA; 24 Manfred Danegger/NHPA; 26
Eero Murtomaki/NHPA; 27t John Shaw/NHPA; 27b, 28,
29t Aquila; 29b Ed Lawrenson; 30t, 30b Aquila; 32 John
Shaw/NHPA; 33 Brian Hawkes/NHPA; 34/35, 35t Peter
Johnson/NHPA; 35b Anthony Bannister/NHPA; 36, 37t,
37b Stephen Dalton/NHPA; 38 Grospas Nature/NHPA;
39t Peter Johnson/NHPA; 39b S. Krasemann/NHPA; 40t
Aquila; 40b Brian Hawkes/NHPA; 41 Fotocentre/NHPA;
42, 43t ZEFA; 43b Aquila; 44 Jany Sauvanet/NHPA; 45t
Aquila; 45b E. Hanumantha Rao/NHPA

Note to the reader
In this book there are some words in the text which are printed in **bold** type. This shows that the
word is listed in the glossary on page 46. The glossary gives a brief explanation of words which may
be new to you.

Contents

Introduction

We share our planet with millions of other animals. We give some of them food and shelter. Some, like horses or camels, can be tamed. Others, like sheep and cattle, are kept on farms. We call these types of animals **domestic animals**. Most animals on earth are wild animals. They have to find their own food and know how to protect themselves.

Places to Live

The place where an animal lives is called its **habitat**. Animals can live in the holes of trees, under pebbles, or high up in a mountain stream. Animals live in every nook and cranny on earth.

Many things affect the habitat of plants and animals. Is it hot or cold? What type of soil is there? Is it in the mountains? Is it close to the sea or **inland**? All these things add up to make the animal's surroundings, which we call its **environment**.

▼ The African elephant lives in hot, dry areas. Its large ears keep it cool.

Elephant seals live in very different surroundings from the African elephants. Their bodies are covered in thick blubber to keep out the bitter cold.

Millions of Types

Millions of types, or **species**, of animals live on earth. Some animals are very tiny and often have only one part or **cell**. An example is the **amoeba** (*am-ee-ba*). The largest animal is the blue whale, which is over 90 feet long!

Each type of animal fits into one kind of environment. Some animals live in hot deserts. A few, like the polar bear, prefer the cold. On Mount Everest, 25,000 feet above sea level, there lives a small bird. At a depth of 25,000 feet below sea level, there lives an unusual fish called a tripod fish. Some places, like coral reefs, attract many more species of animals than others. The greatest mixture of types of animals live in hot, steamy jungles.

All these animals have become used to a life in one kind of place. Their shape, size, color, food needs, and skills have changed over thousands of years to adjust to life in that habitat. This change is called **adaptation**.

Survival in the Wild

▼ A lioness begins to chase giraffes. There is only a small chance that she will catch and kill one of them. The long legs and heavy hoofs of the giraffes could knock the lioness down. The lioness is taking the chance because she needs food. Staying alive is not easy, even for her.

Have you ever been really cold or hungry? The answer is likely to be "no." Most of us eat every day and sleep in our warm beds at night. In the wild, it is not the same. Animals usually have to struggle to find food and shelter. They must always look out for danger. Most animals end up as food for another type of animal.

Staying Alive

Animals defend themselves in many ways. Some animals, like turtles, have a tough armor. Other animals have weapons like the horns of a goat. A few animals, like some tropical frogs, are poisonous. Some pretend to be fierce. The owlet moth has wings with huge "eyes" on them. These

A Natural Order

There is an order in this struggle for life in the wild. This order begins with the sun. Plants use light from the sun to make their food. Animals do not do this. They have to eat plants or other animals.

The sun is the first link in a chain. This chain is called a **food chain**. There are many other links to study. Think of a pond. There are water lilies on the pond. A butterfly takes **nectar** from the lilies. The butterfly is snapped up by a dragonfly. Suddenly, the long tongue of a frog lashes out. It grabs the dragonfly. In the grass nearby lies a snake. The frog is eaten by the snake. Then, like a feathered torpedo, an eagle rushes to earth. The eagle kills the snake after a hard fight.

Most animals in this chain have eaten another animal. The only plant eater is the butterfly. In the end, they all depend on the plant.

▲ Most animals need to keep a lookout for enemies. A rabbit has no defense against an attacker and therefore must either hide or run. Nevertheless, the rabbit family is one of the most successful animal groups. Rabbits breed very quickly and can live in many different climates.

eyes frighten attackers. Deer can run very fast. This allows them to escape from their enemies.

One way of staying alive is not to be seen at all. Many animals blend in with the leaves, the rocks, and the soil around them. Some insects look like twigs. They are **camouflaged**.

Animals that hunt other animals are called **predators**. They have to chase, catch, and kill their prey. The predators need speed, strength, and strong teeth to do this. Look at a cat's teeth. Imagine those daggers twenty times bigger in a cheetah. All is well for a predator until it is unable to catch its **prey**. What happens to a cheetah if it breaks a leg or goes blind?

eagle

snake

frog

dragonfly

butterfly

▲ All life depends on some other form of life for food. Plants supply food for plant eaters. Plant eaters then become meals for meat eaters. Both plant eaters and meat eaters need plants to survive.

Seashore Life

There are many types of seashore. There can be rocky, pebbly, sandy, or muddy shores even along a short stretch of coast. What type of rock is the shore made of? Is it hard or does it crumble? Waves slowly wear away the rock, no matter what type of rock it is. The waves may wash the small pieces of rock, or pebbles, along the coast. The pebbles rub together and break into large sand grains. Flat beaches are formed where fine sand collects.

High and Low Tides

Twice a day, the sea creeps up on to the land and goes back again. This rise and fall is called the **tide**. When the sea reaches its highest point, it is high tide. When the sea is at its lowest point, it is low tide. The tides are caused by the pull of the moon and the sun.

Sandy Beaches

Many small animals live on sandy beaches. If you look into the water at high tide, you may see shrimps, crabs, or jellyfish. They all disappear at low tide. Some burrow under the sand where it is safe. Below the surface the sand stays damp, which is what they like.

This picture shows animals on a rocky shore when the tide is out. Limpets, mussels and barnacles cling to the rocks. A rock pool has become home for a starfish and a shrimp. Sea anemones fan out their tentacles in the pool. Lugworms and cockles bury themselves in the sand. An oyster catcher patrols the beach in search of cockles. It will use its strong beak to break open the cockle shells.

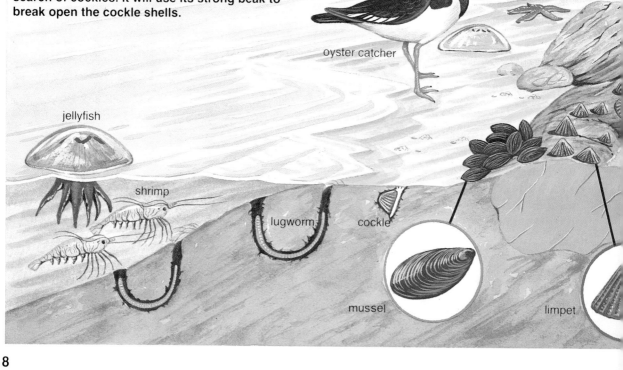

oyster catcher

jellyfish

shrimp

lugworm

cockle

mussel

limpet

► The shore crab, seen here, blends in very well with its surroundings. It is a poor swimmer and spends most of its time crawling through rock pools. It feeds on small animals.

shore crab

starfish

sea anemone

barnacle

Lugworms sift through the sand for food. They leave coils of sand behind them, which you may see at low tide. Wading birds, such as oyster catchers and snipe, walk along the sand. They poke the sand with their long beaks in search of the small animals. They also go through the rubbish, or **debris**, which is left on the beach by the waves.

Rocky Beaches

Rocky beaches have many more species of animals than sandy beaches. At high tide, animals cannot burrow into the sand to escape the crashing of the waves. Therefore, they must have strong shells and be able to cling to the rocks. Some, like mussels and scallops, hang on with tough "ropes." Others, like limpets and barnacles, hang on to the rocks with a wide sucker.

When the tide goes out, small pools of water are left among the rocks. The pools are full of living things. In the rock pools there are small fish and crabs. Sea anemones (*a-nem-o-nees*) cling to the rocks. Starfish move around slowly.

Life in Lakes and Rivers

Water inland is known as fresh water. Fresh water does not contain as much salt as seawater. Most animals who live in water are used to either a life in the sea or to a life in fresh water. A few can live in both. There are many types of habitat in fresh water.

Streams and Rivers

Life in a river changes along its length. A river can be divided into different parts or **reaches**. Reaches often start in the mountains. The upper reach is steep and has boulders. The cold water rushes along and carries small stones with it. There are few plants and animals that can get a grip, but plants called **algae** (*al-gee*) and insect **larvae** (*lar-vee*) cling to the boulders. Only strong fish like salmon can survive.

Water in the middle reach also flows swiftly, but it drops the small stones or gravel. Plants have a chance of getting a grip in the gravel. Most animal life exists where gravel collects. Snails and larvae with flat bodies, like mayfly, live among the plants. Fish, such as trout, live in the middle reach, too. They are strong swimmers and have a good shape for pushing through the current.

In the low reach, the water slows down and warms up. The land is flat and there are no rocks. The river drops fine mud, or **silt**, which it has carried from the mountains. Burrowing in the silt are clams, worms, and turtles. Many plants grow in the low reach. The fish have narrow bodies so they can slip through the plants.

▼ These pictures show some of the life found in a north European river. In the upper reach, salmon and a few insect larvae live in the fast flowing water. In the middle reach, trout, snails, and mayfly larvae are found. In the low reach, fish such as tench and chub are found. Other life includes freshwater turtles, clams, and worms.

UPPER REACH

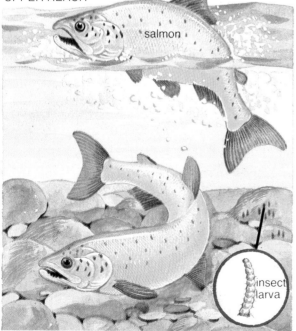

salmon

insect larva

MIDDLE REACH

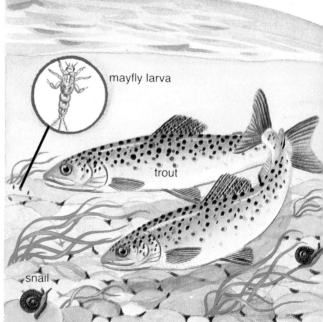

mayfly larva

trout

snail

Labels: dragonfly, frog, plankton, pond skater, water strider, tadpole, sunfish, bass, snail

▲ A wide range of plant and animal life is found in a pond. The water is still, which means that the plants and animals do not have to struggle against flowing water. Tiny plants and animals float near the surface. These plants are food for larger animals, such as bass. The other animals include insects and amphibians.

LOW REACH

Labels: clam, freshwater turtle, worm

Lakes and Ponds

Lakes are larger and deeper than ponds. In the middle of lakes, there is little plant life. A lake can be divided into three sections. On the lake *bottom*, it is cold and dark. Few animals live there. Tiny **plankton** float near the surface. They are eaten by fish such as bass.

The busiest part of the lake is near the *edge*. Plants grow here. There are snails and insects like water striders. Fish with slim bodies, like sunfish, move through the plants.

Ponds are smaller and shallower than lakes. They sometimes dry up. Water plants can grow anywhere in a pond. Ponds attract many animals. Some, like frogs, live in and out of the water. Frogs are **amphibians** (*am-fib-ee-ans*). The frogs return to the ponds in spring and lay eggs in the water. When the young tadpoles hatch, they must grow fast to become frogs before the pond dries up.

11

Life in Wet Lands

Swamps and marshes are areas of wet land. They can be near the coast or inland. Their waters are still, or **stagnant**, and are slightly salty near the coast. Marshes are open, grassy areas. Swamps are like flooded woods. People do not like to make their homes in marshes or swamps. People have drained many wetland areas to make dry land.

▼ A green heron wading in a swamp in Florida. The green heron is about 15 inches long. It is one of the smaller members of the heron family. It dives into the water in search of prey.

Animals that live in these wet areas are very much at home. Many of the larger animals have **webbed feet** to keep them from sinking. Plants, too, have to adjust to a watery life. Although the soil is rich, it is usually flooded.

Life in the Mud

Marshes close to the sea are called **tidal marshes**. Plants, called rushes, grow here. Snails crawl up the rushes. Fiddler crabs dart about and eat as they go. The snails and crabs are eaten by terrapins, a type of turtle, and herons. Herons are wading birds with long legs and wide feet. Their feet stop them from sinking into the mud.

Ducks, geese, and grebes (*gree-bs*) are birds that feed on the grasses and the reeds of freshwater marshes. Grebes are birds with feet like paddles. The **bills** of wading

ibis

flying fox

proboscis monkey

fiddler crab

kingfisher

mudskipper

frog

birds are all shapes. The shapes suit the way they feed. Many birds sift through the mud. Others spear small animals.

There are many newts and toads. Muskrats and large **rodents**, called nutria, run around. Rodents are gnawing animals.

Plants with unusual shapes grow in the swamps. Swamps are often noisy, because of the croaking of the bullfrogs. There are biting insects like mosquitoes. Some swamp animals are dangerous. There are alligators and snakes. One snake, the water moccasin, drops from trees on to its prey.

Lungfish live in hot swamps. If the swamps dry up, the fish bury themselves in **cocoons** under the mud. They stay there until the swamps flood again.

▲ Mangrove swamps are found near the mouths of tropical rivers. There are millions of insects. Larger animals include frogs, leaf-eating monkeys, bats, and birds, such as the kingfisher.

Mangrove Swamps

A mangrove is a tree which grows in the muddy swamps along **tropical** coasts. It has roots which stand above the water.

Little crabs live in the mud. Kingfishers, ibises (*i-bis-es*), and some frogs feed on the crabs. There are few **mammals** in mangrove swamps, but otters, monkeys, and flying foxes can be found. These foxes are really bats.

Mudskippers are fish which live in the hot, steamy swamps. Mudskippers live in the mud above the water. They breathe air through **gills**, which they keep full of water. Mudskippers have to return to the water to feed and breed.

◄ Mudskippers live in water and on land. They grow up to a foot in length. They use their fins to climb out of the water and to move across the mud.

Grasslands of the North

Grasslands are large areas of dry land found on most **continents**. The grasslands lie between the forests and the deserts. **Temperate** grasslands are cool. **Tropical** grasslands are hot. All grasslands are flat or rolling **plains**. There is little rainfall, which means that few trees can grow.

Grass is a tough plant with deep roots. Grass can survive if there is little rain. Animals which eat grass are called **grazers**. Most of the animals on grasslands are grazers. **Predators** attack the grazers. If the grass dries up, the grazers die. Then, there is nothing left for the meat eaters. In the end, all the animals depend on the grass for survival.

Grasslands have few hiding places. Grazers either run fast or burrow to escape from their enemies.

Temperate grasslands are found in Central Europe, the Asian steppes, and the North American prairies.

The Prairies of North America

In the past, life on the prairies was unspoiled. The grass was eaten by bison (buffalo) and pronghorn. Pronghorns are swift runners like antelope. Bison and pronghorn moved across the prairies to find fresh grass to eat. There were many prairie chickens which were eaten by the predators, such as wolves.

▼ A herd of bison grazing in an American national park. Bison do not see well, but they do have a good sense of smell and good hearing. This is very useful if enemies are nearby.

About 100 years ago, people moved on to the prairies. They started to grow crops and rear cattle. They plowed up the tall grass to grow wheat. Further south, the shorter grass plains were also plowed up. They soon turned to dust. Most of the prairie was ruined. What happened to the wildlife? The wolves were poisoned. Now, **coyotes** have taken their place. Millions of bison were shot. Today bison are protected by law.

The Burrowers

Rodents called prairie dogs live under the ground. There, they can avoid predators and the cold. They have a well-run life. Their living area is like an underground town. They have to go above the ground to eat. Some keep guard and watch out for coyotes. Others pull out the weeds. This allows better plants to grow.

▲ Beneath the northern grasslands lies a secret world of tunnels. The prairie dog is one of many small animals that lives underground. It is a relative of the squirrel. It gets its name because it barks like a dog.

▼ Pronghorns can run faster than horses. Therefore, they can escape from most predators. They are always on the alert for danger. Millions of pronghorn used to roam the prairies, but few are found today.

Grasslands of South America

Grasslands cover much of South America. The temperate grassland is called the pampas. It stretches across a vast area of land east of the Andes Mountains. The name comes from the grass which grows there called pampas grass. It is a tall plant like a reed. Much of this grass has been cut to make room for farming.

Burrowers and Grazers

Pampas animals, like the prairie animals, are mostly burrowers and grazers. The burrowers of the pampas include cavies (*cay-vees*) and tuco-tucos (*too-ko-too-koes*).

Cavies are wild guinea pigs. They have no tails, and they look very much like pet guinea pigs. Tuco-tucos have long teeth with which they dig. The tuco-tuco's name comes from the noise it makes.

One pampas rodent, the viscacha (*vis-car-cha*), likes to clear the ground around its burrow. The viscacha then builds up mounds of earth, sticks, and stones which are used as lookout posts.

Grazers include the pampas deer and a bird called the rhea. It is sad that the pampas deer are now rare. Rheas look like small ostriches. Like ostriches the rheas cannot fly. Rheas are fast runners and roam the pampas in flocks.

▼ The pampas deer is one of the few large animals found on the South American grasslands. They graze in pairs or in small herds.

Insect Eaters

The insects of the grasslands include crickets, ants, and **termites**. The insects are eaten by armadillos and giant anteaters. Armadillos have shells of tough, leathery plates. If they are attacked, they curl up in the same way that woodlice do. Giant armadillos, five feet long, have 100 peg-like teeth for crunching insects.

Giant anteaters prefer to eat termites. These anteaters have long, strong claws which they use to tear open termite nests. They have no teeth. Instead, they have a long snout with a sticky tongue which traps the insects. Giant anteaters can grow up to six feet in length.

▲ The long legs of the maned wolf help it to walk through tall grass. It hunts at night and often covers more than 20 miles in search of food. The maned wolf does not run very fast so it hunts quietly and pounces at the last moment.

Predators

Other hunters, or predators, hunt larger prey. The maned wolf eats rodents, birds, reptiles, insects, or fruit. The maned wolf looks very much like a fox, but it is taller and has long legs. Unfortunately, the maned wolf is now rare. Another rare predator is the pampas fox. It has been hunted by people, and there are very few left now.

Grasslands of Africa

Hot, dry grasslands called **savannas** cover much of Africa. Savannas are dotted with thorny trees and bushes. Rain only falls for a few weeks of the year.

Savannas are well known for their wildlife. Life is not easy for the animals.

Camouflage is vital for some. Strength or speed are vital for others. Most of the animals can last a long time without water.

Tree and Bush Eaters

Trees, such as acacia (*a-kay-sha*), are food for many animals. There is a leaf eater for each layer of the tree. Let's take a look at the animals that feed on an acacia from the bottom to the top. Near the ground, we see a dik-dik, which is a tiny antelope. Eating further up is an eland with curly

gazelle

wildebeeste

elephant

zebra

cheetah

rhino

ostrich

African wild dog

lioness

horns. Eating even higher up than the eland is an elephant. The elephant's strong trunk tears the tree to shreds. Eating at the top of the tree is the tall giraffe, which searches among the thorns for tender leaves.

Another large animal, the black rhino, eats the savanna bushes.

Grazers

Most savanna grazers are **mammals** with hooves. Many grazers seek safety in numbers. Herds of 10,000 or more

giraffe

dik-dik   eland

African buffalo

python

wildeebeeste (*wil-da-beest*) and zebras roam the savanna together. Herds of gazelle roam the savanna, too. Gazelles can run at speeds up to 42 mph.

The huge African buffaloes weigh as much as 1,800 pounds. Buffaloes are dangerous when they are angry. If they are attacked by lions, the buffaloes can kill the lions.

Warthogs and white rhinos do not live in herds. They graze alone. Rhinos carry a bird, the cattle egret, on their back. The egret eats **ticks** off the rhino.

One animal that is not a grazer is the ostrich, which is the largest and fastest running bird.

Predators

A well-known hunter is the lion. The females do most of the hunting. They hunt in teams and kill large animals like zebras. Cheetahs are smaller than lions, but they run much faster. Cheetahs hunt alone. They hunt small prey like gazelles.

All animals hate hyenas because the hyenas steal food from them. Large packs of hyenas can drive a lion from its kill. Wild dogs use teamwork when hunting. Although wild dogs are small, a few hunting together can bring down a zebra.

Other meat eaters are baboons, which eat rodents. There are also deadly snakes, which eat meat. Huge pythons squeeze their victims to death. The victims can be as large as an antelope!

◀ The savanna grasslands of Africa are home to many different animals. Many of these are the biggest and best of their type. The African elephant is the largest of all land animals. The giraffe is the tallest animal. The cheetah is the fastest running animal. The ostrich is the tallest and fastest running bird. There are huge herds of wildeebeeste and zebras. All these animals have to share the hot, dry environment with many other animals.

Grasslands of Australia

The savanna grasslands of Australia lie between vast areas of desert and tropical forests. They have less rain than the savanna grasslands of Africa. During the day, it is very hot, and the dry winds blow often. Many of the mammals sleep through the heat of the day and come out only at night. They are known as **nocturnal** animals.

Mammals with Pouches

In most of the world, mammal babies grow inside the mother. In Australia some mammal babies grow outside the mother in a pouch. Mammals with pouches are called **marsupials** (*mar-soup-e-als*).

▲ A frilled lizard putting on a display to frighten its enemies. Although its gaping mouth and wide collar makes it look rather frightening, the lizard is harmless.

Some marsupials do not look like other mammals. Kangaroos have large back legs which they use for jumping. Kangaroos are grazers, and some of them can hop at speeds of up to 30 mph. The wombat is another grazer. It comes out at night to feed. During the day, it sleeps in its burrow.

Another animal that burrows is called the echidna (*i-kid-na*), or spiny anteater. The echidna is one of the few mammals that lays eggs. The young echidna hatch in a pouch and then feed from the mother.

Not many meat eating mammals are found in the savanna grasslands. There are, however, a few marsupial cats found in the open savanna woodland, although they are more common in the forests. One meat eating mammal that is found in the savanna grasslands is the Australian wild dog called the dingo. It usually hunts in packs.

◄ Red kangaroos in the Australian outback. When kangaroos stand still, they use their tails for support. You can see a young kangaroo in the mother's pouch in the picture.

Other Animals

Although termites are tiny insects, they can build mounds that are taller than a person. Many thousands of termites live in these mounds. There are other insects, like grasshoppers, and **reptiles** like frilled lizards.

Frilled lizards are only eight inches long and look like tiny dragons. When the frilled lizards are angry, they open their mouths and spread their frilly collars. This behavior scares their enemies. Other reptiles include tiger snakes, which are like cobras.

Colorful birds live in the savanna. The budgerigar (*budge-ree-gar*), which is always green in the wild, lives close to water holes. Bright blue mulga parrots are found also. The emu is an ugly bird with scruffy feathers. It is a large bird that does not fly. not fly. Wedge-tailed eagles, the largest eagles in the world, have wing spans of over six feet. They eat small marsupials.

▼ Water holes on the dry savanna are always busy places. Predators know this and wait near the water for their prey. The budgerigars flap noisily to confuse predators that might be nearby.

Animals in Rain Forests

Forests cover many parts of the earth. They vary from cold pine forests to the hot steamy jungles. Another name for jungles is **tropical rain forests**. There are rain forests in Asia, Africa, Australia, and South America. Rain forests are found close to the Equator. The Equator is a circle which goes around the middle of the earth. The land area close to the Equator is always hot and wet.

Rain forests are full of plants and tall trees which like hot climates. There are beautifully colored flowers and twisting vines, as well as mosses and ferns.

Many animals are found at every level of the forest. Bats and birds are at the top. Tree climbers are in the middle. Small animals are on the ground.

▼ A tropical rain forest can be divided into three layers. Different kinds of animal live in each layer. At ground level, small animals live in the thick undergrowth. A greater number of animals live in the trees of the middle layer. Above this, the tops of the taller trees spread out to form a roof, or canopy, of leaves and branches. The top layer is home for many bats and birds.

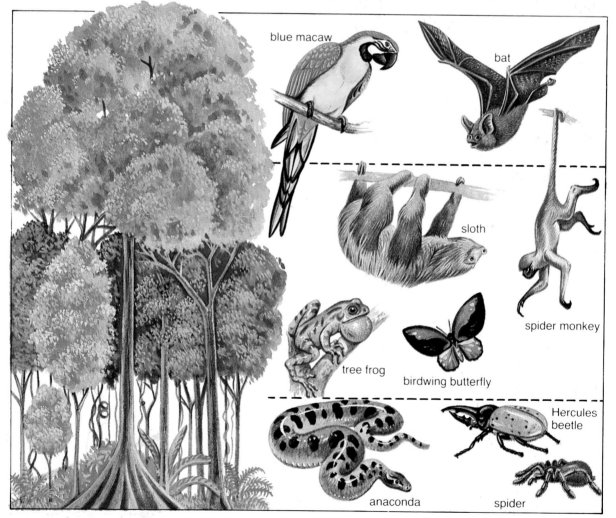

blue macaw

bat

sloth

spider monkey

tree frog

birdwing butterfly

Hercules beetle

anaconda

spider

Climbing Animals

Animals that do not fly have to be good climbers. They need to climb to reach the fruit and flowers in the trees. They need good eyesight, too. Good eyesight helps them to leap from branch to branch.

One of the best known groups of climbers is the **primate** group. This group includes apes and monkeys. Apes and monkeys have better brains than most animals. They also have hands with thumbs. Their hands are useful tools which help them to grip branches. Some monkeys, like the spider monkey, use their tail as an extra arm.

Many primates are clever. Large red Asian apes called orang utans know how to find food. They figure out which trees have fruit by watching the movements of birds.

Other climbers include sloths and koalas. Sloths are slow-moving plant They are only found in South America. Koalas live in Australian forests and they have sharp claws.

▲ A young orangutan hanging by its hands and feet. Orangutans have a thin coat of red hair. Parts of their bodies are hairless, and their grey skin can be seen. Orangutans are found in the forests of Borneo and Sumatra.

Other Animals

Rain forests are full of interesting animals. In South America, there are huge insects like the six inch long Hercules beetle. There is also a spider which grows up to ten inches across. In New Guinea, there is a butterfly called the birdwing, which has a wingspan of twelve inches.

Frogs like wet, warm, or **humid** places. Some are tiny and colorful. Many are poisonous. Tree frogs have sticky pads on their feet in order to cling to smooth trees.

Reptiles, too, are found in the rain forests. Anacondas, which are large snakes up to 21 feet long, strangle their prey. Other **predators** include members of the cat family. Bengal tigers are found in Asia, and jaguars are found in South America.

Animals in Woodlands

The hot, wet rain forests are found in the **tropics**. The tropics are lands that are close to the Equator. As you move north or south of the tropics, and therefore get further away from the Equator, you come to cooler lands. These lands are called the **temperate zones**.

In the temperate zones, there are forests and woodlands. They are found in North America, Asia, and Europe. Temperate woodlands have cold winters and hot summers. These changes that occur during the year are known as the **seasons**.

The seasons have a strong effect on woodland life. Many trees shed their leaves before the winter. They do this to guard against the cold. In the spring, things start to grow again. Small bushes and plants burst into life. The plants have to grow quickly before the leaves of the trees block out the sun.

▼ A red deer stag. Red deer are found in the woodlands of North America and Europe. The males, or stags, have bony antlers which drop off each spring. New antlers grow in the summer.

Food all Year Around

In the growing seasons, animals eat the plants. Plant food includes buds, leaves, flowers, fruit, and nuts. In the winter, there is little to eat. Some animals, like squirrels, store food for the winter. Others get as fat as they can and then rest during the winter. Their body fat keeps them alive.

Small **mammals** include mice, shrews, and hedgehogs. They eat plants and insects. The small mammals are prey for badgers, raccoons, and foxes. These like meat, but they also eat plants.

In the past, bison and boar grazed in the woods. Today, few bison and boar are found because people chopped down the trees and shot the large animals. Black bears still survive in North American woods. The most common large animals are the deer.

▲ A selection of woodland mammals. The black bear and the raccoon are found only in North America. The hedgehog and the European badger are found only in Europe. Squirrels and mice live in all woodlands.

Life in the Trees

Look closely at a tree. You will see ants and beetles. Caterpillars move slowly through the tree and eat the leaves. Some insects, such as gall wasps, live in little red "balloons," called **galls**, which they build on leaves.

Birds of many kinds can be found in woodland trees. Flycatchers are birds that eat insects. Their beaks have bristles which trap insects. Other birds, like cardinals, have short beaks for cracking nuts. Owls are meat eaters. Their beaks are curved and pointed for tearing flesh.

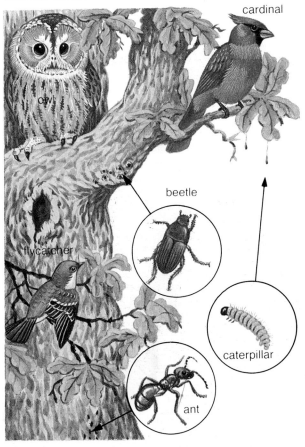

◀ A woodland tree, such as the oak, is home for thousands of small animals and birds. These include beetles, ants, owls, and flycatchers. Cardinals are found only in North America.

Animals in Pine Forests

Pine forests stretch across Canada, Alaska, northern Asia, and Europe. They lie north of the temperate woodlands. The summers are short and mild. The winters are long and harsh.

Pine trees can survive the cold winters. Their leaves are like tough needles. The trees do not bear flowers or fruit. Instead, **cones** protect the seeds. Trees that have cones are called **conifers**. They include fir, spruce, and pine trees. Most conifers are **evergreen**. This means that their leaves do not all fall off at once. Conifer forests are dark and shady all year around. Ground plants below conifers hardly grow. The forest floor is too thick with dead needles.

Warm Coats

Some animals, like the moose and brown bear, are found right across the northern forests. All the mammals in the north have thick fur for warmth. Many of these animals, like the mink, sable, and beaver, have been hunted for their fur.

Mink live by the water and eat fish and **rodents**. A much larger relative of the mink is the wolverine. It is a strong, fearless hunter. Other hunters include the wolf and the lynx. The lynx is a strong, stocky cat with ear tufts. The lynx has large feet to stop it from sinking into snow. Brown bears, including huge grizzly bears, live here, too.

Plant eaters include beavers and moose. Beavers have webbed feet and are at home in water. The moose is a large animal up to six feet tall at the shoulder. Because moose find little food in the winter, they have to eat the bark from the trees.

Birds and Insects

Few reptiles and amphibians live this far north. They have no fur or feathers to keep them warm.

There are fewer types of insects in pine forests than in woodlands. What insects there are in woodlands are found in great numbers. Spruce bark beetles and wood wasps live in pine trees. The female beetles make holes in the tree trunks, into which they lay their eggs. The young insects stay in the tree until they are adult. Wood wasps only lay eggs in dead or dying trees.

Insects are food for birds like creepers and warblers. The most well-known insect eaters are woodpeckers. Their beaks cut tunnels into tree trunks. Then, their long, sticky tongues reach into the tunnels and trap ants.

A bird called the crossbill has a scissor-shaped beak. It uses its beak to open pine cones. Hunting birds include the bald eagles and the fish eating ospreys.

◀ Brown bears are some of the largest meat eaters. This picture was taken from the safety of a tree. What the photographer may not have known is that hungry bears can climb trees.

▲ A moose with a calf. This calf is nearly one year old. Moose calves are born in May or June. They stay with their mother until she produces another calf. The moose is the largest of all deer.

▲ The bald eagle of America. This is a famous bird of prey. It is skilled at swooping down to catch fish which come to the surface of lakes and rivers.

Life in the Coldest Places

Beyond the forests of the north lies the **tundra**. The tundra is the coldest land area of the north. The ground is frozen most of the time. During the short summer, the earth **thaws** a little. Then, plants have a chance to grow in the boggy soil. The plants include heathers and grasses.

Beyond the tundra lie the Arctic Ocean and the North Pole. The Arctic is usually frozen solid. In the summer, some of the ice breaks up into moving chunks called icebergs. The North Pole is always frozen.

At the opposite end of the world is the South Pole. The South Pole is on a large area of land called Antarctica. This land is covered with thick ice. Very few plants grow there.

The North

Plant eaters on the tundra include lemmings, musk-oxen, and caribou. The other name for caribou is reindeer. Musk-oxen have long, shaggy coats for warmth. They are heavy animals that stand stand five feet tall. Small animals, like lemmings, are food for weasels, Arctic foxes, and snowy owls. Wolves hunt the musk-oxen and caribou.

Polar bears live on the tundra during the summer. In the winter, they live on the Arctic ice. There they can hunt seals. Seals and walruses live in and out of the water. Thick fat protects them from the cold. Seals and walruses are **sea mammals**. Other sea mammals are the whales. Unlike seals and walruses, whales always stay in the water. White belugas and narwhals are Arctic whales. Narwhals have a long tusk which looks like a unicorn's horn.

▲ The polar bear is the biggest and strongest predator of the far north. It is seen here in the summer on land, where it searches for any kind of food that it can find. During the winter, it lives on the Arctic ice and hunts seals. The male hunts alone. The female hunts with her cubs.

The South

Most of the animals which live in Antarctica are birds. There are few plants for them to eat. They depend on the sea for their food. Many types of birds can be found living near the sea.

One of the birds which nests in Antarctica is the albatross. Albatrosses spend most of their lives roaming the oceans. They are the largest living birds, with wing spans of nine to ten feet.

Penguins are very different birds from the albatrosses. Penguins use their wings for swimming instead of for flying. Their torpedo-shaped bodies make them good divers for fish. The largest penguins are the Emperor penguins. They are over three feet tall. The males use their bodies as nests. They stand over the eggs to protect them. Sometimes, they stand in blizzards for weeks while the females search for food.

Different seals have different diets. Leopard seals eat penguins. Weddell seals are fish eaters. Crabeater seals eat tiny shrimps, called krill.

▲ A Weddell seal with a pup. The Weddell seal is very clumsy on land, but it is sleek and fast in the water. It can dive to a depth of 2,000 feet in its search for food.

▼ These Emperor penguins normally move on land by using their short legs. If alarmed, they move off by tobogganing on their bellies.

Animals that Hibernate

Some animals find it hard to live in the winter. The cold and lack of food are big problems. Food supplies are hard to find. In the winter, many trees shed their leaves. Animals who like eating leaves have to eat the bark of trees instead. Nut eaters have few problems. Nuts are easily stored for winter use.

If animals stop moving, they need very little food to keep alive. Therefore, if food is lacking in the winter, some animals **hibernate**. This means that they have a long sleep. Before sleeping, they eat as much as they can to get as fat as possible.

All mammals and birds can make their own heat. They are called **warm-blooded** animals. All other types of animals are **cold-blooded**. They cannot make their own heat. The weather controls their body heat. They like to live in warm places.

▲ A hibernating dormouse. This winter sleep lasts from late October until April. During this time, the dormouse does not move, and its breathing is very slow.

▼ A black bear hibernating. The bear does not sleep as heavily as the dormouse. The bear wakes from time to time, but it will still not eat or drink for months.

Warm-blooded Sleepers

There is only one bird that hibernates. This is a little American bird called the poor-will. All other warm-blooded sleepers are mammals.

Some mammals, such as bears, badgers, and chipmunks, sleep for short periods. From time to time, they wake up to feed. This is not deep hibernation. Other mammals go into a deeper sleep. Their breathing and heart beat slow down, and their body heat drops. While they are in this deep sleep, their body fat is used to keep them alive. They do not wake up until the spring comes. Small mammals like dormice, hedgehogs, and ground squirrels are deep sleepers. They often sleep curled up to keep warm.

Cold-blooded Sleepers

Frogs are cold-blooded. They hibernate in the winter as well as some other times. Cold-blooded animals are only active if they are warm. If there is a cold spell in the summer, their bodies cool down. Then, they have to rest. Some mountain frogs have to rest for eight months!

Frogs sleep under dead leaves or in the mud at the bottom of ponds. Painted frogs and natterjack toads are examples of deep sleepers.

Reptiles which hibernate include wall lizards, pond turtles, and small snakes called asps. Some asps live in the mountains of Europe. They rest in large groups. They make nests under the ground, beneath stones or in hollow trees.

The winter can be very hard for pond animals, especially when the surface freezes. Some animals, such as freshwater turtles, frogs, and some fish, bury themselves in the muddy bed of the pond. They hibernate until the warmer weather comes.

beetle

stickleback

frog

insect larva

freshwater turtle

tench

Mountain Animals

The further up a mountain you go, the colder it gets, and the growing season is shorter. Finally, you get to a point where plants cannot grow at all.

Mountain life has many problems. The winds are strong. The high mountain air has little **oxygen**. Oxygen is a gas that all living things need. Both animal and plant life have to survive steep, rocky slopes.

Most mountain plants have short stems. Plants with long stems would be blown down by the wind. Many mountain plants are shaped like spongy cushions, which helps the plants keep warm. Their flowers are brightly colored to attract as many insects as possible in the short summer.

Most animals spend the summer in the high mountain meadows. As the winter approaches, and their food becomes scarce, they go down to the lower valleys.

▼ The mountain goat spends most of its life high up in the mountains. The mountain goat lives in small groups and feeds on plants.

▲ Alpine choughs are found on the highest mountains in the world. They feed on insects and worms and live in flocks of about 20 birds.

Sturdy Climbers

Plants often grow on places which are hard for animals to reach. Mountain animals must be able to balance on ledges. European chamois (*sham-wa*) have rough hoof pads to keep them from slipping. Their American cousins are mountain goats, which have thick, woolly, white coats.

Vicunas (*vi-coon-yas*) are rare animals which live in the Andes Mountains. Vicunas belong to the camel family. Vicunas are found up to 18,000 feet on mountains. Their blood can hold more oxygen than normal blood. This helps vicunas to deal with the thin mountain air.

Pikas are small mountain mammals that are like rabbits. Their feet have hairy soles, which grip well. They are like farmers.

They collect grass and then dry it in the sun. The grass turns into hay, which the pikas use for winter food.

Mountain hunters include pumas and snow leopards. Pumas are large cats. They were once common in America, but they are now rare. Snow leopards live in Asia. They prey on wild goats.

Birds and Insects

There are few flying insects in the mountains. They cannot fly in the strong winds. Beetles, grasshoppers, and low-flying butterflies are found in the mountains.

Mountain birds, like eagles and condors, are **soaring birds**. They float on the strong air currents which push up from below. Eagles kill small **mammals**. Condors are huge American **carrion birds**. They eat dead meat, but they never kill. Condors are very rare because many of them have been shot.

When Mount Everest was first climbed in 1953, men saw alpine choughs flying at 24,000 feet. No other bird has been seen at this great altitude.

Desert Animals

Many people think of deserts as being hot, dry, empty places. All deserts are dry, but not all of them are hot.

Clouds act like blankets. They keep the earth warm at night and cool in the day. Without clouds, hot deserts quickly heat up in the daytime. Nights are cool. The daytime heat escapes quickly into the sky. This happens because there are few clouds.

It hardly ever rains in deserts. Therefore, plants have to survive long periods without water. When it does rain, desert plants burst into life. They take in as much water as they can. Many desert plants have thick, waxy leaves to stop water from escaping.

Heat, Food, and Water

There are several ways that desert animals cope with the heat and lack of water. During the heat of the day, many small mammals keep cool by staying in their burrows. At dawn and dusk, mice, jerboas, kangaroo rats, and other small animals come out in search of food.

The bodies of some animals are shaped to keep them cool. Fennec foxes and jack rabbits have huge ears. The ears pass the animals' body heat to the air like radiators. This keeps the animals cool.

Some desert animals, like the kangaroo rat, never have to drink. All the water they

A herd of springbok. These animals live in the hot, dry regions of southern Africa. There used to be vast herds of springboks, but today they are becoming rare.

▲ The fennec fox is the smallest of all foxes. It lives in the dry lands of Africa. It feeds on lizards, insects, and small rodents.

need comes from the food they eat. Their bodies do not sweat. Therefore, water is kept inside their bodies as long as possible.

Larger mammals like camels can go for long periods without drinking. When they find water, they drink large amounts. The smaller oryxes (*or-ixes*) with long pointed horns also seldom drink. They get water from the plants they eat.

Reptiles and Insects

Many reptiles and insects are found in hot deserts. These animals like warm places. They do not lose much water through their dry skins.

One type of bug, called a coccid (*kok-sid*), covers itself with a waxy coat if no rain comes. It stays like this for many years. When rain eventually falls, the insect comes to life again.

Reptiles are at home in the desert. Lizards and snakes are a common sight, although they avoid the burning heat if they can. Some, such as sand boas and dune vipers, burrow in the sand. They are the same color as sand, which makes them hard to see. They prey on small desert mammals.

▼ A sand-diving lizard. This lizard wriggles through the sand like a snake and pushes itself along with its strong back legs. It searches for insects beneath the surface.

Animals of the Night

Most people are active by day and then sleep at night. In the wild, there are many animals that sleep during the day and are awake at night. These animals are called **nocturnal** animals.

Why do some animals live by night? In the desert, many animals sleep through the day because of the heat. They can move around at night without getting too hot. Also, the night is safe for many animals. In **tropical rain forests**, insects and small frogs are safe from birds at night because most birds are asleep. Hunting animals also like to move at night. They move quietly, unseen, and creep up on other animals that are fast asleep.

On the Prowl

Most cats, large and small, like to hunt by night. Like many night animals, cats have good night sight. They can see six times more in the dark than people can see. The leopards of Asia and Africa are night prowlers. They hunt small antelopes called duikers. Jaguars in South America hunt small deer called pudus, which are only one foot tall. The only cat that does not hunt at night is the cheetah.

Another night prowler is the shy aardwolf, which is a member of the hyena family. The aardwolf's tongue is long and sticky in order to lick up the termites which are its favorite food.

Some animals **scavenge** at night. These animals include foxes, badgers, and jackals. They search for scraps of food. This is easier than hunting live animals. Foxes and badgers sometimes raid garbage cans.

Night Senses

As well as having good sight, animals of the night need other **senses**. Good hearing is important. Owls have very good hearing. They can find their **prey** on the darkest nights just by listening. Smell is also useful. The aardwolf finds termites by smell. Kiwis from New Zealand hunt for worms by smell. Their nostrils are at the end of their long bills.

Bats are well-known night animals. Bats are flying mammals. Their sight is not good. Instead, they find their way around in a very unusual manner. If you shout in a large cave you will hear an **echo** of your voice. The sound of your voice bounces back off the walls. Bats have learned to use echoes to find their way. This is called **echolocation**.

▲ A European badger on the prowl at night. Badgers like to scavenge for food. They also hunt small animals like frogs, toads, snails, and mice.

▲ Owls are night hunters. Their soft feathers hardly make a sound as the owls fly through the air. Both their eyes face forward, which means that owls rarely miss their prey when they swoop in for the kill.

► Bats flying in search of food. The picture shows how the wings are made of flaps of skin which are stretched over a framework of thin bones. The bones are like very long fingers.

Animals on the Move

So far, we have looked at all sorts of **environments**. We have also looked at the animals that live in these places. Many animals, however, do not stay in one place. They make long journeys at certain times of the year. Their journeys are called **migrations**.

Why do animals migrate? There are a number of reasons. When the **seasons** change, the weather changes. If the weather becomes too cold, some animals move to warmer places. Other animals move when their food supply runs out. **Grazers**, for example, move to fresh grasslands. They will return after new grass has grown again.

Many birds migrate long distances to **breed**. Other animals, like some fish and turtles, also migrate across oceans to breed.

Long Journeys

During the summer, caribou feed on the small plants of the **tundra** in Alaska. As winter comes, the caribou gather in large herds to move south. The caribou herds always use the same routes. They travel 600 miles or more to find warmer grazing grounds.

In Africa, the savanna grasslands dry up if there has been no rain. Animals such as zebra and gnus travel long distances in search of fresh grass and water.

Small animals migrate, too. Army ants march across forests and cause a lot of damage as they go. Some types of butterflies and moths migrate to warmer places. Monarch butterflies fly from Canada to Mexico to avoid the winter. They move back north in the summer.

▼ A huge herd of wildebeeste and zebras crossing a river in Tanzania, Africa. The rainy season is over, and the rivers and land will soon dry up. The animals are migrating westward in search of fresh grazing land. They will return when the dry season is over and the grass has grown again.

Record Breakers

Nearly half of the birds in the world migrate. It is easy for them to escape the winter because they can fly. Birds which migrate include terns and plovers. The Arctic tern is a record breaker. It spends one summer in the Arctic. Then, it flies over 10,800 miles to spend another summer in Antarctica. Golden plovers fly from the northern tundra to the pampas of Argentina. During the trip, they can fly up to 480 miles in one day.

Fish migrate, too. Salmon are born far upstream in rivers. When they are older, they swim to the oceans. The salmon live in the oceans until it is time to breed. Then, they return to the streams and rivers where they were born.

◄ These migrating cranes breed in the marshy areas of northern Europe and Asia. They are moving south as the winter approaches in order to avoid the cold.

▼ Caribou on their long journey south. Caribou can stand the cold better than most animals. They move south to find food as well as to escape the cold.

Animals on Islands

Islands can be any size from a few hundred feet to hundreds of miles across. Islands are land surrounded by water. Some islands are near land. Other islands are in the middle of oceans.

The islands in the middle of oceans are a long way from the rest of the world. Some islands have no people on them. This means that animals can live on these islands without being disturbed. Only certain types of animals are found on these islands. Most land mammals and **amphibians** are not found there. They cannot swim across the oceans to reach the islands. Many types of insects are also not on the islands. Reptiles find these far off islands hard to reach. The most common island animals are birds.

▲ A small island crowded with gannets.

▼ Seabirds are usually the first animals to reach newly formed islands. Seagulls were among the first to arrive on Surtsey, a volcanic island off Iceland, that rose out of the sea in 1963.

A Safe Home

Birds flock to islands to breed. Some islands become very crowded. The bird nests almost touch each other. Gannets, gulls, boobies, and terns are examples of birds that crowd on to islands to breed. They are safe there. How do these island birds find food? The answer is that most island birds are seabirds. Seabirds get their food from the sea.

The Galapagos Islands in the Pacific Ocean are a safe home for the animals that live there. Giant tortoises, five feet long, and iguanas are found there. Iguanas are huge lizards, up to six feet long. The tortoises and iguanas are reptiles. If they had to compete with mammals for food on the islands, they would not be very successful.

▼ Relatives of this tuatara once lived all over the world. The few that are left live on a few islands off New Zealand. Tuatara feed on snails, insects, and other small animals.

Some Dangers

People do not live on many **remote** islands. When people do settle on these islands, they upset the **native** animals that live there. People bring other animals with them such as dogs, cats, goats, and even rats. These animals upset or kill the animals already living on the islands. Most island animals cannot fight back.

One type of island bird, the dodo, once lived on an island called Mauritius in the Indian Ocean. The dodos could not fly, which made them easy to catch. By 1680, so many dodos had been killed that none were left. They are now **extinct**.

Today, we try to be more careful. Island animals are protected by law. Reptiles called tuataras are found only on an island off New Zealand. Tuataras look rather like clumsy lizards. They are protected and have been saved from extinction. They have lived on earth for over 200 million years.

Taming Wild Animals

When the first people hunted for food, they had to travel long distances. Later, people kept animals so they did not have to hunt. They gave food to the animals. When the animals were fat, they killed them. This is how the first farm animals known as cattle were tamed. Cattle today rely on people. They could not live in the wild for very long.

People have kept animals for thousands of years. Animals that people keep are known as domestic animals. They are kept for many reasons. Some are kept for their milk, some are kept for their wool, and some are kept for their meat. Other animals have been taught to help people. They have been used to carry people and goods for hundreds of years.

Animal Helpers

Horses are animals that help people. They can carry a rider over 50 miles in one day. Each horse has to be trained to obey a rider. Horses are quick to learn. They can also be trained to pull wagons and carts.

In developed countries, cars and trucks are now used to carry loads. However, there are still some places like mountain trails that cars and trucks cannot reach. There, animals are needed. In some

▼ The horse is a valuable helper. Rounding up cattle on horseback is hard work, but rounding up cattle on foot would be a lot harder.

underdeveloped countries, many animals are still used to carry heavy loads. Cars and trucks are much more expensive to keep. In Asia, elephants are trained to lift heavy loads like tree trunks.

Some birds can be tamed to help people. Falcons are birds that have been used for a long time to hunt rabbits. Pigeons can be be trained to carry messages. They can fly long distances with a message.

Animals help **disabled** people. Small monkeys are trained to help feed people who cannot use their hands. Dogs are other animals that are useful. Guide dogs are trained to help blind people. Other dogs are trained to help find criminals or to stand guard.

Our smallest helpers include bees and silkworms. Silkworms are young insects that spin silk thread. We take the silk thread and then make clothes with it. Bees have given us honey and wax for thousands of years. The bees work very hard for us. All we do in return is to give them beehives in which to live.

▲ Camels have been used for thousands of years to carry heavy loads over great distances. Camels are bad tempered and need careful handling.

▼ Peregrine falcons are birds of prey which can be trained to help people hunt small animals.

Wildlife in Danger

There was life on earth long before the first people lived. We know this from the study of rocks and **fossils**. The fossils tell us that many types of animals, which are no longer found, once lived. Some of these early animals, like the dinosaurs, are well known to us.

The study of rocks tells us that the earth is always changing. For example, we know that places which are deserts today were once covered by sea. We also know that the weather on earth has changed through the ages. If animals cannot cope with the changes on earth, they die out or become **extinct**. Scientists think that the dinosaurs died out because the earth changed from being hot to being cold. The dinosaurs could not adjust to these changes. Other animals can deal with change. Many types of insects found today lived on earth long before the dinosaurs.

Animals also die out because new animals enter their **habitat** and kill them. A famous island bird, the dodo, became extinct this way. It could not defend itself against the animals that people brought to its habitat.

▼ Leatherback turtles lay their eggs in nests which they dig in sandy beaches. Once the eggs are laid, the female returns to the sea. Local people dig the eggs up and sell them in the markets. The number of leatherbacks is going down because so many eggs are dug up and sold.

▲ A Siberian white crane, which is one of the rarest birds in the world. Many cranes have been shot because of the damage they do to crops. Their nest sites have also been turned into farmland.

The Dangerous Human

The most dangerous animal of all is the human. We kill millions of other animals each year for their meat or skins. We kill other animals just because the animals are a nuisance.

There are now strict laws about hunting. The tiger is an example of an animal that used to exist in great numbers. People hunted the tiger so much that now there are very few tigers alive.

People have made many changes on the earth. We have cleared forests for farming. We have built cities, factories, and roads. This development has left many animals with noplace to live. This activity has often left the world spoiled. A lot of waste is produced from our factories and cities. Some of the waste is poisonous, which puts wildlife in danger.

We are now aware that much animal life is in danger of extinction. If a habitat is destroyed, animals that live there have to be moved to safety. Wildlife parks have been set up around the world to provide animals with safe homes.

There are some 350 types of birds in danger around the world. Many of these birds live on islands. One is the Galapagos hawk. These hawks are found only on the Galapagos Islands. Their lives were disturbed when people came to live on the islands. Many were shot and their food was eaten by other animals. Now the hawks are protected by law.

Groups of people all around the world now take care of animals. It may be too late to save some of the animals in danger. We are beginning to understand that the world belongs to every living thing.

▼ Tigers once lived in jungles throughout Asia. Experts believe that there are less than 3,000 tigers in the wild today. Although they are protected by law, hunters still kill them for their valuable skins.

Glossary

adaptation: the way in which a plant or animal slowly changes to survive in different surroundings.

algae: very simple plants. Algae have no leaves, roots, or stems.

amoeba: a tiny, simple animal which lives in water. An amoeba has no fixed shape.

amphibian: an animal which begins its life in water but lives on land when it is adult. Frogs, toads, newts, and salamanders are amphibians.

bill: the beak of a bird.

breed: to produce young.

camouflage: the colors, patterns, or shapes which help an animal to hide by blending in with its surroundings.

carrion bird: a bird which eats dead animals. Carrion birds do not kill animals for food.

cell: a very small part or unit of living matter. People are made up of millions of cells.

cocoon: a case which a young animal forms around itself for protection.

cold-blooded: describes animals which cannot make their own heat. The temperature of their bodies depends on whether the weather is hot or cold. Insects and reptiles are cold-blooded animals.

cone: the part of a conifer tree where seeds form.

conifer: one of a group of trees which have needle-like leaves. Conifers produce woody cones to protect their seeds.

continent: a large mass of land. The earth is divided into seven continents.

coyote: a wolf-like animal. Coyotes are found in North America.

debris: the remains of something which has been broken or destroyed.

disabled: describes an animal, person, or object which is weakened or not working properly. A fox with a broken leg is disabled.

domestic animal: describes an animal which has been tamed. Domestic animals are no longer wild.

echo: the sending back of a sound. Echoes are caused by sounds bouncing off a hard object.

echolocation: a way of finding objects by sending out sounds and then listening for the echo. Bats use echolocation to find their prey.

environment: the surroundings of an animal or plant. The environment affects the way an animal lives.

evergreen: describes trees and bushes which are in leaf all year. Evergreen trees do not drop their leaves when the cold weather comes.

extinct: describes a type of plant or animal which has died out.

food chain: a chain of living things which depend on each other for food. A typical food chain starts with a plant which is eaten by a plant eating animal. The plant eating animal is then eaten by a meat eating animal.

fossil: the remains of an animal or plant, which is usually found in rocks. A fossil can be the bones of an animal or the shape left by the animal's body in the rock.

gall: a growth on a plant caused by an insect.

gill: the part of a water animal used for breathing underwater. Most animals with gills cannot breathe out of water.

grazer: an animal which feeds on grass.

habitat: the place where an animal usually lives.

hibernate: to "sleep" or stay still through the winter. Animals hibernate in order to survive through the cold weather and when food is scarce.

humid: describes moist or damp air. A place is humid when the air contains a lot of moisture.

inland: area of land located away from the coast.

larva: an early stage in the life of certain animals. Larvae look different from adults. Tadpoles and caterpillars are larvae.

mammal: a warm-blooded animal which is usually covered in fur. Mammals give birth to live young which feed on the mother's milk.

marsupial: a mammal which has a pouch on the outside of its body. The young develop in the pouch.

migration: the movement of animals over long distances to find food, to breed, or escape from cold or dry weather.

native: describes an animal or plant which naturally belongs to a place. Penguins are native birds of Antarctica.

nectar: a sugary liquid that plants produce in their flowers. Many insects visit flowers to feed on nectar.

nocturnal: describes animals which are active at night.

oxygen: a gas found in the air. Oxygen is very important to all plants and animals. It is used in breathing.

plain: a large, open area of flat land. Plains are usually covered in grass.

plankton: tiny groups of plants and animals which float near the surface of sea and inland waters. Plankton is a source of food for many water animals.

predator: an animal which hunts and eats other animals.

prey: an animal which is caught and eaten by other animals.

primate: a member of a group of mammals which includes apes, monkeys, and people.

reach: a part or stretch of a stream or a river. The low reach, for example, is the part of a river closest to the sea.

remote: describes something which is far away, or distant. A remote island is a long way from other land.

reptile: a member of a group of animals which includes snakes, lizards, crocodiles, and turtles. All reptiles have dry, scaly skins and lay eggs with shells. Reptiles cannot make their own body heat.

rodent: a member of a group of small animals with long front teeth which are used for gnawing. Mice and squirrels are rodents.

savanna: a hot, dry grassland with few trees.

scavenge: to feed on waste or on the remains of food left by other animals.

sea mammal: a mammal which lives in the sea. Because sea mammals breathe air, they must come up to the surface to breathe. Sea mammals include whales and dolphins.

season: one of four periods of time during the year. The seasons are spring, summer, fall, and winter. Each season has a certain type of weather.

sense: one of the body's natural powers which enables an animal to be aware of its surroundings. The five senses are sight, hearing, touch, smell, and taste.

silt: very fine rock grains which are carried along by a river. When the silt drops to the river bed, it forms mud.

soaring bird: a bird which flies high up in the sky without having to move its wings.

species: a group of animals or plants which look alike and can breed with one another. It takes two adults of the same species to produce young.

stagnant: describes water that is still. Stagnant water is often full of plants. As the plants rot, they give off an unpleasant smell.

temperate: describes a climate which has summers that are almost never too hot and winters that are almost never too cold.

temperate zone: refers to a part of the world which has a temperate climate. There are two temperate zones. They are between the tropics and the polar regions.

termite: a type of insect, similar to an ant, which lives in large groups or colonies. Termites feed on wood and can cause a lot of damage to buildings.

thaw: to raise the temperature of something above its freezing point so it becomes liquid. When ice thaws, it becomes water.

tick: an animal which is related to spiders. Ticks attach themselves to warm-blooded animals and suck their blood.

tidal marsh: a flat, grassy area found near the sea at the mouth of a river. The soil is rich and muddy and often covered by sea water.

tide: the regular rise and fall of the sea up and down the shore. There are two high tides and two low tides every 24 hours.

tropical: describes something to do with the tropics or coming from the tropics.

tropical rain forest: a very hot, damp forest found in the regions close to the Equator. Tropical forests are covered in tall trees and plants.

tropics: the very hot, damp regions of the earth which are found close to the Equator. The Tropic of Cancer marks the most northern line of the tropics and the Tropic of Capricorn marks the southern line.

tundra: a treeless plain found close to the arctic regions. The tundra is frozen for most of the year.

warm-blooded: describes an animal which can keep its body at a steady temperature. It does this by making its own heat. A warm-blooded animal can lose heat if it gets too hot.

webbed feet: describes the type of feet which many water birds have. Webbed feet have toes joined by a layer of skin, which helps the animal paddle through water.

Index